Gover...
Rea...

1050 L

GAYLORD FG

King Henry VIII

King
Henry VIII

By Robert Green

A First Book

FranklinWatts

A DIVISION OF GROLIER PUBLISHING

New York London Hong Kong Sydney

Danbury, Connecticut

Visit Franklin Watts on the Internet at:
http://publishing.grolier.com

Library of Congress Cataloging-in-Publication Data

Green, Robert, 1969–
King Henry VIII / by Robert Green.

p.   cm.—(A First book)
Includes bibliographical references (p. 58) and index.
Summary: A biography of the English monarch who challenged
the Pope's authority, established a state religion, married six wives, and
presided over the beginnings of the Renaissance in England.
ISBN 0-531-20305-0
1. Henry VIII, King of England, 1491-1547—Juvenile literature. 2. Great Britain—
History—Henry VIII, 1509-1547—Juvenile literature. 3. Great Britain—
Kings and rulers—Biography—Juvenile literature. [1. Henry VIII, King of
England, 1491-1547. 2. Kings, queens, rulers, etc. 3. Great Britain—History—
Henry VIII, 1509-1547.] I. Title. II. Series.
DA332.G77   1998
942.05´2´092—dc21
[B]   97–10988
                                                                      CIP
                                                                      AC

Contents

I

ENGLISH ROSES AND TUDOR KINGS

Around 1526, Henry VIII, King of England and Ireland, became smitten with a nineteen-year-old woman named Anne Boleyn. Anne had been raised at the French court, and Henry wrote to her in French proclaiming his devotion:

> *My mistress and friend, I and my heart put ourselves in your hands, begging you to recommend us to your favor, and not to let absence lessen your affection to us.*
> *. . . Seeing I cannot be present in person with you, I*

send you the nearest thing to that possible, that is, my
picture set in bracelets . . . wishing myself in their place,
when it shall please you.

Anne refused to live with Henry without a formal proposal of marriage. Henry would have liked to propose to
her; unfortunately, though, he already had a wife, Catherine of Aragon, and divorce was not an arrangement recognized in Catholic England. The pope in Rome, the
supreme leader of the Catholic Church, would not allow it.

Henry grew restless. Catherine had failed to give the
king a male heir who could carry on his family's rule and
prevent civil war in England. Although Catherine had
given birth to a daughter, Mary, on February 18, 1516,
no queen had ever ruled England. It was a common belief
that no woman had the right to rule.

Henry tried to force matters in May 1527. He met with a council at the house of his principal adviser, Thomas Wolsey. There the king and his men began secret proceedings to secure a divorce from Catherine. Wolsey wanted them to appeal to the pope to dissolve the marriage. But Henry thought that he could have his divorce without the pope. He wanted to seek the support of

The death of Richard III at the Battle of Bosworth put an end to the long War of the Roses. Henry Tudor triumphed and was crowned King Henry VII in 1485.

wealthy antichurch aristocrats in England—and join with general antipapist sentiment—in sweeping away the old religion and securing a divorce on his own terms.

When Catherine heard about the secret meeting, she burst into tears. Realizing that the pope would not consent, Henry looked toward more extreme measures. It had become clear that Henry was strong-willed, but few expected him to become so bent on absolute power that in his lifetime he would challenge the authority of the pope; bring a new religion to England; marry six wives; and preside over the beginnings of the Renaissance in England.

Henry was born at Greenwich on June 28, 1491. His parents, King Henry VII (called Henry Tudor) and Elizabeth of York, were members of two powerful and opposing families, the House of Lancaster (Henry Tudor) and the House of York (Elizabeth). Henry VIII's lifelong desire to establish a clear line of succession and avoid civil war had its roots in the history of his father's England.

On August 22, 1485, King Richard III of England was slain in a battle against Henry Tudor at Bosworth Field. Richard was a member of the House of York, whose family emblem was a white rose. The family emblem of the House of Lancaster was a red rose.

From 1455 to 1485, the two families fought for control of the English throne in what came to be known as the War of the Roses. England suffered from disorder and hardship as the English throne passed back and forth between Yorkists and Lancastrians. When King Henry VII was crowned in 1485, he decided to marry Elizabeth of York, hoping to bury the blood feud by bringing the white rose and the red rose to flourish under the same roof.

The defeat of Richard III and Henry VII's marriage to Elizabeth did end the War of the Roses. But the peace of the resulting years—the years of Henry VII's reign— was fragile.

The Yorkists threatened revolt from time to time, as did other pretenders to the throne. A child of mixed blood (Lancastrian and Yorkist) would represent the only hope for a lasting peace. Henry was greatly relieved, therefore, when Elizabeth gave birth to two sons, Arthur (Henry VIII's older brother) and Henry. The offspring of the two families would rule as the House of Tudor.

After the War of the Roses, the English people hungered for a strong king. They desired peace, prosperity, and order. And by the end of his reign, Henry VIII had become such a colossal figure that he seemed to have one foot in England and one foot on the continent of Europe, where England, once isolated and weak, had become a competing power.

During the 1400s, while England was divided by the War of the Roses, the rest of Europe was energized by the dis-

The marriage of Henry VII, pictured here holding
the red rose of the Lancastrians, to Elizabeth
joined the houses of Lancaster and York and
prevented further war between the two sides.

Christopher Columbus appeals to Spain's King
Ferdinand and Queen Isabella on April 17, 1492,
for support in his quest to find new shipping routes
in the Atlantic Ocean. The "New World" that Columbus discovered brought vast wealth to the Spanish.

coveries of the Renaissance. It was a time, following the Middle Ages, when Europe experienced a rebirth of ideas and a renewed interest in the teachings of ancient Greece and Rome. The Renaissance first sprang up in Italy and gradually moved throughout Europe.

The Renaissance stimulated international trade and scientific curiosity, and it sparked a new interest in exploration. Europe began to look to the great world beyond, hungering for wealth, knowledge, and power.

In 1492, one year after the birth of Henry VIII, Christopher Columbus, in the employment of King Ferdinand and Queen Isabella of Spain, sailed for a vast uncharted land mass in the Atlantic Ocean. The "New World," or the Americas, as these lands came to be known, yielded undreamed-of wealth to European explorers. For many years, the kings of France and Spain had been the great powers in Europe. But as the vast wealth of the Americas flowed into Spain and Portugal, the traditional balance of power in Europe began to shift.

England at first took little part in this great struggle for world power. Henry VII was busy rebuilding his kingdom after the War of the Roses. But during his reign, the king's shrewdness and industry swelled the royal treasury. Prosperous and at peace, England suddenly found itself eager for a share of the power in Europe.

Henry VII decided to seal an alliance with Spain's King Ferdinand by marrying his eldest son, Arthur, to Catherine of Aragon, Ferdinand's daughter. The kings of England and Spain both wanted to isolate King Louis XII of France, who was a little too powerful for their comfort.

In 1502, less than five months after the kings of England and Spain had joined their children to upset their French enemy, Arthur died. Suddenly, the attentions of the court fell on Arthur's younger brother, Henry. The little red-headed prince Harry had always lived in his older brother's shadow. Now he could show off for his new admirers.

Henry was the first English king to be brought up under the influence of the Renaissance. His youthful days were divided between studies and sports. Private tutors taught the prince to read Latin (the language of the ancient Romans, still used as an international language in Henry's time), French, Italian, and Spanish. The poet John Skelton tutored him in English composition and grammar. Skelton also taught young Harry how to behave like a prince, with confidence and dignified manners.

From an early age, Henry showed a special interest in religion. He debated questions of theology (the study of religion) with church officials. England at that time was a Catholic country, and Harry prided himself, perhaps above all else, on being a faithful Catholic.

Arthur, Prince of Wales, married Catherine of Aragon, the daughter of King Ferdinand, to seal an alliance between Catholic Spain and Catholic England.

When not studying, Henry delighted in the favorite sports of the time. He hunted, rode horses, shot with a bow and arrow, and learned to fight with a sword and to joust with a lance. He also loved to dance and play music. Henry excelled at music and even composed religious songs called hymns; some of his hymns are still sung in English churches.

In order to preserve the alliance between England and Spain after Arthur's death, Henry and Catherine became engaged. They needed the blessing of the pope because it was unusual for someone to marry his brother's wife. Pope Julius II sent his official blessing in 1504, and

Young Prince Henry suddenly began receiving a great deal of attention after the death of his brother, Arthur, in 1502.

Catherine quietly settled in England to wait for Henry to reach a suitable age for marriage—Catherine was eighteen years old, and Henry was just turning twelve.

In 1509, before Henry was old enough to marry Catherine, an event of the greatest importance occurred: King Henry VII died. The seventeen-year-old prince Harry was crowned Henry VIII King of England in April of the same year.

It was the first peaceful and undisputed succession since 1422. The new king was quick-witted and strong, and he represented all the promise of England's new role in European politics. Moreover, he was determined to put aside his childhood games and apply himself, as his father had done, to the duties of governing England.

Although their marriage was arranged for
political reasons and Henry was six years
younger than Catherine of Aragon, Henry was
genuinely enchanted by the Spanish princess.

II

THE RISE OF CARDINAL WOLSEY

Henry VIII had some of history's most promising tutors to guide his youthful thoughts. But great men are often men of great ambition, and Henry was more likely to trust his own judgment than that of his learned tutors.

One of Henry's early friends and greatest teachers was Sir Thomas More, a prominent thinker of the English Renaissance. More was steeped in the wisdom of the ancient Greek and Roman philosophers and the early

Sir Thomas More opened up young Henry's mind to a whole new realm of ideas in science, philosophy, politics, and the arts.

teachers of the Christian church. He was also fascinated by the discoveries of Arab scientists; the Arabs in the Middle East experienced a great age of learning and expansion while Europe was obscured in the Dark Ages.

Henry loved to debate the mysteries of the universe with More. The two could often be found strolling about, deep in conversation. Sometimes, in the dark of night, they would be discovered on top of a church tower studying the movements of the stars or discussing the nature of God.

They shared a deep devotion to Catholicism. But unlike Henry, More also believed in some of the humanist ideas sweeping through Europe with the Renaissance.

This humanism shifted the focus of people's musings from religious subjects to more earthly debates. Observation of the laws of nature inspired new scientific inquiry, and study of the arts, philosophies, and political practices of the Greek and Roman classical age became prominent.

One idea that worried More was capital punishment, or the execution of criminals. Young prince Harry was probably amused as More argued for compassion for convicted criminals. Henry, on the contrary, would come to rely more and more on the chopping block to quiet his enemies. When he took the throne in 1509, Henry beheaded two of his father's chief advisers.

Thomas More must have grimaced at the cruelty of the executions. The prince, who still loved to debate theoretical questions like a scholar, quickly proved himself to be a swift and remorseless political realist.

Henry VIII believed that a king's will should be obeyed above all other laws. During the Renaissance, many of the monarchs in Europe came close to wielding complete control over their subjects, and others dreamed of such supreme power.

In England, the chief limitation on the king's powers was the availability of money, which was controlled by Parliament—a constant thorn in the side of the Tudor monarchs. Kings were also limited by the threat of revolt from unhappy subjects and by the laws of the Church.

Despite his love of power, Henry came to rely upon his advisers, as most kings did, for the day-to-day running of the country. In time, one man came to dominate Henry's early reign more than all others, and that was Cardinal Thomas Wolsey.

The ambitious Cardinal Wolsey was delighted to see that Henry's early reign was taken up looking for a bride, leaving much of the real power in his hands.

Wolsey, the son of a butcher, had begun his career as a humble priest in the Catholic Church. But he was so shrewd and so ambitious that he soon gained recognition in the Church and in the royal court. Wolsey kept abreast of the events of Europe. He knew how much depended on the delicate alliances between various nations in Europe, and he dreamed that England would play a larger role in determining the future of the Continent. Wolsey also dreamed of becoming pope.

Despite Henry's pledge upon coming to the throne to concentrate on matters of state, he was quickly swept up in wedding arrangements; many important matters fell into the hands of Wolsey. The marriage of Henry to Catherine of Aragon was arranged for political reasons, but Henry seemed to be very much in love with her. They married in a chapel in Greenwich on June 11, 1509.

Pleased with his new bride and his position as king, Henry hungered for some adventure worthy of a young king of England. An ambassador from the Italian city of Milan remarked that he was "as eager for war as a lion." In 1512, Henry joined his father-in-law, Ferdinand II of Aragon, in an attack on France.

France had long been a threat to the lands in Italy controlled by the pope. Moreover, the French threatened to dominate Europe. Henry was deeply devoted to the pope and fought against the French in the name of the Church.

Henry showed great bravery at the Battle of the Spurs in France. Then, in the summer of 1513, the English army laid siege to and occupied the French towns of Therouanne and Tournai. (The towns were returned to France in peace negotiations a short time later).

While Henry was in France, an army loyal to the Scottish king, James IV, attacked England. England and Scotland were not united, as they are today. In the king's absence, the defense of the realm was left in the hands of Thomas Howard, Earl of Surrey. The earl rushed Henry's forces northward and defeated the invading Scots at Flodden Field. The war with the Scots proved to be much more important than the war in France. Among the dead at Flodden Field lay the body of James IV.

Henry sorely regretted missing the battle against his Scottish neighbor, but his exploits in France were popular with the English people. The greatest

The different colors in this map show the boundaries of the clans, or extended families, that occupied Scotland during the time of Henry VIII. The warlike Scots and their allegiances with the French posed a constant threat to Henry's England.

This Scottish soldier in full armor brings the bitter news back from Flodden Field that their king, James IV, has been slain in battle against the English.

victor of all was Wolsey, who had gained Henry's confidence by planning the campaign against France. Wolsey soon became indispensable to the king. By 1515, Wolsey was Archbishop of York, Lord Chancellor of England, and a cardinal (high official) of the Catholic Church.

Henry, believing that Wolsey had a firm grasp on government matters, grew more and more concerned with producing an heir for the English throne. After several stillbirths, Catherine gave birth to a daughter, Mary, in 1516, but the unhappy king wanted a male heir. He began to look around for other women who might bear him a son.

Henry took a mistress named Bessie Blount. She did, in fact, become pregnant with Henry's son. They named the child Henry Fitzroy (which means king's son). Fitzroy later became Duke of Richmond and Lord High

Cardinal Wolsey lived in lavish style. His home, Hampton Court, was much like a palace, and many people felt that he acted too much like a king.

Admiral of the English Navy. But he could not be considered an heir to the English throne because he was not a child of a legitimate marriage.

Meanwhile, Wolsey was deeply involved in European politics. He had become so powerful that many European ambassadors directed business to Wolsey in place of the king. They believed that Cardinal Wolsey ran England while King Henry delighted only in games and women.

Wolsey lived in grand style in places like Hampton Court, his London residence, but he never had the delusion that he was king. When Henry was finally convinced that Catherine would not provide a male heir, he pressed Wolsey to secure the pope's approval for a divorce. It proved more difficult than either Henry or Wolsey had imagined to get the pope to agree. Henry's attempt to divorce Catherine of Aragon became known as "the king's great matter," so much did it consume his attention. Wolsey's failure to secure the divorce had unforeseen and dramatic results, not only for himself and Henry but for all of England.

III

"THE KING'S GREAT MATTER"

Henry came to believe that his marriage to Catherine of Aragon was unjust in the eyes of God. The curse of the frequent miscarriages arose, thought Henry, from a Biblical passage in the Book of Leviticus that forbids a man to marry his brother's wife: "If a man takes his brother's wife, it is impurity; he has uncovered his brother's nakedness, they shall be childless." (Leviticus 20:21)

When Martin Luther posted his Ninety-Five Theses on the door of the Castle church in Wittenberg, Germany, in 1517, he challenged the Catholic Church, the most powerful institution in the Western World.

Henry believed this warning, even though the pope had sent his approval for the marriage of Catherine and Henry after Arthur's death. While the officials of the Church in Rome debated the question of Henry's divorce, the status of the Church elsewhere in Europe was rapidly changing.

In 1517, a young Catholic priest named Martin Luther nailed a long list of complaints to the door of a chapel in Wittenberg, Germany. Luther protested against the Catholic Church's role in politics and against the vast wealth that the pope had accumulated. Most of all, Luther took offense at Catholic priests' practice of selling indulgences, or promises of forgiveness and salvation. Luther did not believe that Christians should be trying to buy their way into heaven.

The tiny tremor caused by Luther's action soon rumbled into an earthquake, and Europe found itself shaken by a broad movement, called the Reformation, that changed Christianity forever. The Reformation is the starting point of a number of breakaway sects—such as the Lutherans, who followed Luther—that became known collectively as the Protestant Church.

Germany was the center of the Reformation, but reformers could be found in all the countries of Europe. In 1521, Henry, still devoted to the pope, published a short book entitled *The Assertion of the Seven Sacraments Against Martin Luther* that denounced Luther. The pope was so pleased with it that he rewarded Henry with the title of Defender of the Faith; Henry swelled with pride.

Like Henry, Cardinal Wolsey was distressed by the Reformation. He dreamed of a peaceful Europe in which England could play a larger role. He had been working for years to arrange a number of grand alliances between England and the great powers of the European continent. The Reformation threatened to undo his plan.

Wolsey had negotiated the Treaty of London in 1518, temporarily ending the war with France. And in 1519, when the Holy Roman Emperor Maximilian died, Wolsey plotted for Henry to be named emperor. There was no more chance of Henry becoming emperor than of Wolsey becoming pope, but the king and his minister pressed their claims with optimism.

The nineteen-year-old Charles V, of the Hapsburg dynasty in Germany, was elected emperor. Charles inherited a vast empire including Spain, Holland, Belgium, Austria, Hungary, Bohemia, Milan, Naples, and Sicily. Wolsey turned his attention instead to the king of France, Francis I, who found himself isolated by the vast influence of the new emperor. Wolsey arranged a meeting between Henry and Francis I. In June 1520, the two kings met in Flanders in northern France at a place that came to be known as the Field of the Cloth of Gold.

Henry and Cardinal Wolsey had great
appetites for power—one hoped to become
Holy Roman Emperor and the other Pope.

The kings of England and France, Henry VIII and Francis I, met amid such splendor that the meeting place was called the Field of the Cloth of Gold.

The meeting was as splendid as could be imagined. Thousands of Englishmen accompanied Henry to France. Francis received Henry with lavish entertainments and a makeshift royal residence. The two kings promised each other eternal friendship and behaved like two old school chums. One day they even had a wrestling match, in which Francis threw the more athletic Henry to the ground; Henry was very embarrassed.

The meeting at the Field of the Cloth of Gold was one of Wolsey's greatest moments. He watched with pleasure as the kings enjoyed themselves. But in reality, the displays of friendship between Francis and Henry proved to be empty. By 1523, Henry had entered into an alliance with Emperor Charles V. Henry and Charles immediately declared war on France. English troops were not sent into battle, but Henry sent money to support the costly war.

In 1525, a battle was fought at Pavia in northern Italy, where Francis received a firm rebuke by Charles's

Although the Battle of Pavia was fought between the Holy Roman Empire and France, England sent funds to support the Empire. The success of the imperial forces undid Cardinal Wolsey's plans for English supremacy in Europe.

imperial forces. But the real loser was Wolsey: He had been passed over for the supreme position of pope in 1523; his dream for a peaceful Europe proved elusive; and after 1525, England neared bankruptcy from the expenses of the war. Wolsey and Henry were forced to raise taxes in England. Henry, whose popularity suffered with the levying of new taxes, grew more impatient with Wolsey every day.

Henry ordered Wolsey to make peace with the French—the war was simply too costly. In August 1525, the Treaty of the More was signed, ending hostilities between France and England. But the king still wondered why Wolsey, who could form difficult alliances between foreign leaders, had still not secured permission from the pope for Henry to divorce Catherine.

Moreover, at the Field of the Cloth of Gold, Henry had been charmed by a sophisticated young girl named Anne Boleyn. Anne first arrived at the royal court in 1522, by which time Henry's affections for his wife had dried up.

Anne refused to become Henry's mistress. Henry, therefore, became all the more eager for a divorce from Catherine. If Anne would not be his mistress, she would be his wife—but first must come the divorce. At Henry's bidding, Wolsey spent more and more time pursuing "the king's great matter." The pope, however, ignored Wolsey's efforts.

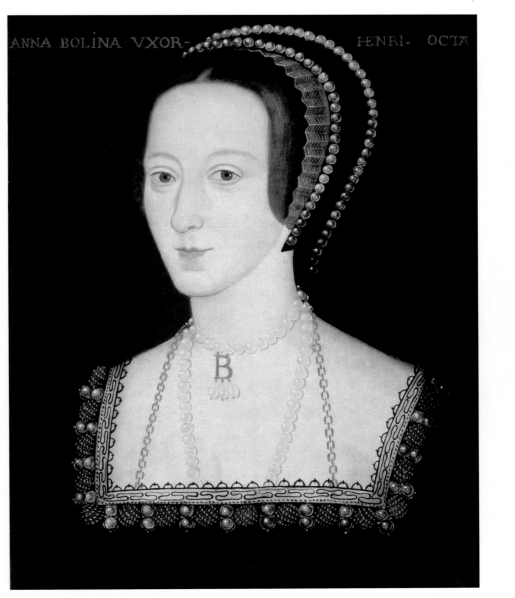

Anne Boleyn

All of the weight of Henry's problems fell on Wolsey's shoulders. He was blamed for England's lack of money, for the failed foreign policy (which brought neither peace nor wealth), and for the failure to secure Henry's divorce from Catherine of Aragon. The English people had always hated Wolsey, and in his days as chancellor he had made many powerful enemies.

Henry decided that the cardinal had to go. As suddenly as Wolsey had risen to power, he fell from the king's grace. Henry confiscated Wolsey's residence at Hampton Court. On November 4, 1530, the king's men arrested Wolsey for treason. Knowing Henry's temperament, Wolsey surely must have expected to be executed. On November 29, however, on the road to his own trial, Wolsey cheated the executioner by dying a natural death. Henry, still determined to have his divorce, drifted toward more drastic measures.

IV
THE BREACH
WITH ROME

After Wolsey's death, Henry looked around for a new chancellor and decided on Sir Thomas More, his old friend. More, unlike Henry, still held on to his scruples and his youthful idealism. He resisted Henry's appointment at first, but when Henry told him that he could always express his feelings openly, More accepted the job of chancellor.

From the outset, More told Henry that he did not approve of a divorce from Catherine. More was a devout Catholic and did all that he could to fight against Luther and the Reformation. For the two years that More was

On Henry's orders, royal troops seized the aging
Sir Thomas More after he refused to swear the
Oath of Supremacy, part of a law allowing Henry
to divorce his first wife, Catherine of Aragon.

chancellor, the king's policies were marked by confusion.

Henry finally realized that he had made a mistake in appointing More as chancellor. More was dismissed in 1532. Thomas Cromwell inherited all of More's power, although he was not given the title of chancellor. Cromwell had served under Wolsey but had very different plans for England.

Cromwell marked the final demise of support for the Catholic Church in England, and he acted quickly. He devised a revolutionary plan to give the king his divorce and reinvigorate England: He would bring the Reformation to England. If the Catholic Church would not grant Henry a divorce, counseled Cromwell, then England would have its own church. But Henry had serious reservations. Had he not always been a good Catholic? Had he not been proud when the pope named him Defender of the Faith? Had he not written a book denouncing Luther as a heretic?

Despite his qualms about abandoning the old faith, Henry grasped at the one great temptation in Cromwell's policies: complete control for the king in every matter concerning his subjects. Henry and Cromwell appealed to the House of Lords and the House of Commons (the two houses that form the English Parliament) for support for the break with Rome. When Parliament resisted,

Henry and Cromwell used all their influence to bully Parliament into agreement.

The matter was brought to a head when Henry discovered that Anne Boleyn was pregnant. Henry could wait no longer. On January 25, 1533, he and Anne secretly married. For a while, the king was husband to two wives. The religious reforms—which clearly made Henry uneasy—now had to be brought to a swift conclusion.

The Archbishop of Canterbury (a large cathedral town in southeast England) had always held the highest rank among the clergy, or religious officials, in England. Cromwell and Henry appointed a new archbishop, Thomas Cranmer, in 1533. Cranmer's loyalty lay with Henry, not with the pope. He was, therefore, the ideal man to aid in the formation of the Church of England, also called the Anglican Church.

In May 1533, Cranmer ruled that Henry's marriage to Catherine contradicted the laws of God because Catherine had been married to Henry's brother, Arthur. The divorce was finally at hand, sanctioned not by the pope but by an official of the new Anglican faith.

By June 1533, Henry had Anne crowned queen of England. English citizens booed the royal procession. Some even cried, "God save Queen Catherine." Many believed that Anne had bewitched Henry.

Thomas Cranmer, Archbishop of Canterbury, was the highest ranking religious official in England. When Cranmer agreed to nullify Henry's marriage to Catherine of Aragon, the church in England had to break with Rome.

The pope reacted with a flurry of denunciations and excommunications. Excommunication formally denies a Catholic participation in the sacred rites of the Church. Cranmer and the bishops loyal to him were excommu-

Pope Clement VII denounced the actions of Henry and Cranmer, and the Catholic priests in England who remained loyal to the pope suffered terribly for it.

nicated first, then Henry. Henry and Cranmer paid little attention to the pope.

The pope's condemnation of Henry and Cranmer did, however, make a difference to many English priests who remained loyal to the Catholic Church. Henry and Cromwell resorted to bullying the English priests just as they had bullied Parliament. By this time, Parliament had fallen in line with Henry's wishes. In 1533 and 1534, Parliament rapidly passed laws to overrule the clergy and strengthen the position of the king.

The two most important laws passed by Parliament gave Henry complete independence from Rome. The first, the Act of Appeals (1533), denied any English priest the right to appeal to Rome on religious questions. The second, called the Act of Supremacy (1534), named Henry VIII Supreme Head on Earth of the Church of

England. Henry had, in the end, followed the way of Luther, and England became a Protestant nation.

Some priests refused to recognize Henry's new authority. When threats failed, Henry resorted to his favorite argument—the executioner's ax. Among many others, John Fisher, the priest who had defended Catherine throughout her divorce trial with Henry, lost his head.

Devoted Catholics are forced to watch as Cromwell's men pillage their abbey. Riches seized from Catholics in England flowed into the state treasury and financed many of Henry's projects, such as the building of the English navy.

Thomas More, who had once counseled Henry against the cruelties of capital punishment, was asked to take an oath of allegiance to Henry and to denounce the pope. More's conscience would not allow him to do it. He, too, died on the chopping block, just after uttering the words, "I die the king's good servant, but God's first." The heads of Fisher and More were stuck on pikes and displayed in London as a warning to others who considered opposing Henry VIII.

As a final insult, Cromwell, with the help of Cranmer, confiscated the wealth of the old Catholic monasteries in England, transferring it to the state treasury. This was the feather in Henry's cap. Not only did he have his divorce and establish his own church, but he grew rich doing it.

V

THE AGING BRIDEGROOM

enry may have reached the height of his powers during the years of Cromwell's guidance: The throne was strengthened against Parliament; the English Church with Henry as its leader broke from the Catholic Church; and money confiscated from the Catholic monasteries flowed into the state treasury. But the king was increasingly restless about his marriage to Anne Boleyn.

Anne had given birth to a daughter, Elizabeth (later Queen Elizabeth I), on September 7, 1533. But Henry still wanted a son to carry on the Tudor bloodline. Henry took up the people's accusation that she had

As King Henry became older, he became more and more concerned about who would succeed him. His daughter Elizabeth, who would eventually become queen, was the child of Henry's second wife.

bewitched him. Divorce proceedings were soon in progress. Henry had brought a religious revolution to England to have a divorce from Catherine and marry his beloved Anne Boleyn. Now he wished to rid himself of Anne as well.

Catherine died on January 8, 1536, still devoted to Henry. On May 19 of the same year, Henry's executioner hacked Anne's head from her body. All the way to the chopping block, Anne proclaimed her innocence and her devotion to the king.

Archbishop Cranmer dutifully pronounced that Henry's marriage to Anne was nullified in the eyes of God. Just two days after Anne's execution, Henry announced that he was engaged to be married to a young maiden named Jane Seymour.

Henry had grown crueler as he aged. He had also grown rather fat. But he was not beyond the grasp of

Jane Seymour

infatuation, or perhaps even love. Romance still occupied more of his thoughts than politics. Above all, Henry still needed a son to rule England after his death.

On May 30, 1536, Henry married Jane Seymour. Jane, the daughter of one of the king's knights, was much younger than Henry. On October 12, 1537, Jane gave birth to a son. He was named Edward and immediately became heir to the throne of England. Jane was not as fortunate: She did not recover from childbirth and died when Prince Edward was not yet two weeks old. Henry was thrilled with his new son and soon decided to take another wife to mother the child.

For the next three years, Henry shopped for a bride. Portrait painters were dispatched to foreign courts to paint the eligible maidens. Henry reviewed the paintings at court while his ministers argued for or against the particular political values of the candidates. The entire affair must have been both comic and disgusting. Cromwell favored a marriage with the German princess Anne of Cleves, sister to the Duke of Cleves.

Cromwell had become alarmed at the 1538 truce between France and the Holy Roman Empire. Francis and Charles had decided to call a truce in an attempt to stamp out the Reformation in Europe. They would not succeed, but the threat alone forced Cromwell to seek

Young Edward VI, Henry's only son, became king at age nine and promoted the Protestant church in England, but he was feeble and only lived to age fifteen.

alliances with Protestant leaders in the duchies (or small states) of Germany.

Cleves was one of the important German duchies. The painter Hans Holbein—who painted many of the surviving portraits of Henry—was sent to Germany to paint Anne of Cleves. When Henry viewed the painting, he was delighted.

It was this portrait of Anne of Cleves that convinced Henry that she should be his next wife. When the unfortunate woman landed in England, Henry was furious that she looked nothing like her portrait.

Cromwell had some hand in fooling the king about Anne's appearance, and the heavily veneered picture convinced Henry. When Anne of Cleves landed in England in the winter of 1540, the king rushed out to see her. He was appalled to see a homely maiden who looked nothing like her picture.

Henry did not even try to conceal his disappointment. "If I had known as much before as I know now," he said, "she should never have come into this realm." But the alliance with the German duchy was important. Anne had traveled a long distance and could not simply be sent home. On January 6, 1540, Henry made Anne his fourth wife.

Henry had grown so accustomed to dispatching wives, however, that this one was sure to go. His wrath fell on Cromwell, even as he flirted with one of Anne's maids of honor, Catherine Howard. Henry told Cromwell to arrange for a divorce from Anne. Cromwell failed to act quickly enough for the king; he undoubtedly wanted Henry to settle down with Anne for political advantages.

But Cromwell should have remembered Wolsey's fate when he tried to interfere with the king's marriages. In a fit of rage, Henry had Cromwell arrested. The great minister was falsely accused of treason and beheaded in July 1540. As soon as the ax had fallen, Henry was overcome with regret.

The course Cromwell had set for England (unlike Wolsey's) had brought independence and wealth to Henry. For the remaining seven years of Henry's life, his policies suffered from a lack of guidance. Cromwell was sorely missed.

Nevertheless, as the Supreme Head on Earth of the Church of England, Henry arranged his own divorce from Anne of Cleves. Just six months after their marriage, on July 7, 1540, the matter was declared at an end. Henry's relationship with Anne, however, lingered on. The divorce was cemented on friendly terms, and Anne remained in Britain. Later, Henry and Anne would often dine together. Nevertheless, on July 28, Henry married nineteen-year-old Catherine Howard.

Catherine Howard was full of life and flirtatious. Partly to celebrate the marriage and partly to assess loyalty in the region, Henry and Catherine set out for the north of England for a four-month state visit called a "progress."

Henry hoped to meet with the Scottish king, James V. The Scots had long been enemies of the English, and Scotland forged alliances with France to threaten the English from the north. Henry hoped to make some sort of peace with the Scots but never made it to Scotland.

Catherine Howard

KATHARINE PARRE

When Henry returned to London, Cranmer displayed evidence to him that Catherine Howard had taken up relations with a man named Thomas Culpeper. The king could hardly believe his ears. He wondered how his wife could prefer another man, so vain had he become.

Despite his vast cruelty, Henry wondered until his last days why so many people had wronged him. His increasing feelings of persecution were vented on Catherine Howard, who was executed in the Tower of London on February 13, 1542.

Henry VIII married one more time, but for convenience, not love. Catherine Parr, his sixth wife, provided some domestic happiness for the aging king. She gathered Henry's three children under a single roof and treated them like her own. She even engaged Henry in discussions about religion—she was deeply devoted to the Protestant Church.

Despite the calm produced by a peaceful, if loveless, marriage, Henry knew that he was growing old. He wanted to die with the knowledge that his children would succeed him on the throne of England. He listed the order of succession for his three children: first Edward, then Mary, then Elizabeth. He still had to fight against

Catherine Parr

claims for the throne from rival families until his death. King Henry VIII died on January 28, 1547.

Henry VIII is most often remembered as the king who had six wives. Their fates are easily remembered with the help of these words: "Divorced, beheaded, died, divorced, beheaded, survived." But through his quest for an heir, Henry laid the foundation for modern England.

He inherited a throne weakened by the War of the Roses. But under his guidance, the position of the king was strengthened. He established a national religion for England and broke away from the pope in Rome.

Henry gave the English people a sense of pride and nationalism. He lives today as a symbol of the greatness of monarchy. The true flourishing of his reforms came not in the reign of the son for whom he had wished but in his daughter Elizabeth's reign. The fears about a female monarch were unfounded. During the Elizabethan Age, England protected its independence with military victories, while poets and playwrights sang the praises of an England made strong by King Henry.

For More Information

Dwyer, Frank. *Henry VIII*. New York: Chelsea House, 1988.

Newcombe, D. G. *Henry VIII and the English Reformation.* New York: Routledge, 1995.

Snowden, Keith. *Katharine Parr, Our Northern Queen.* Pickering, England: Castledon Publications, 1994.

Williamson, David. *Debrett's Kings and Queens of Britain.* Topsfield, Mass.: Salem House Publishers, 1986.

For Advanced Readers

Cannon, John and Ralph Griffiths. *The Oxford Illustrated History of the British Monarchy.* New York: Oxford University Press, 1989.

Fraser, Antonia. *The Wives of Henry VIII.* New York: Random House, 1993.

The Love Letters of Henry VIII. Edited by Jasper Ridley. London: Cassell, 1988.

Seward, Desmond. *The Wars of the Roses: Through the Lives of Five Men and Women of the Fifteenth Century.* New York: Viking Press, 1995.

Smith, Lacey Baldwin. *Henry VIII: The Mask of Royalty.* Chicago: Academy, 1987.

Internet Sites

Due to the changeable nature of the Internet, sites appear and disappear very quickly. Internet addresses must be entered with capital and lowercase letters exactly as they appear.

The Yahoo directory of the World Wide Web is an excellent place to find Internet sites on any topic. The directory is located at:

http://www.yahoo.com

The Tudor England site contains details on the lives of Henry VIII and his wives, the other monarchs of the Tudor Dynasty, life in England at the time, and links to other related sites:

http://tudor.simplenet.com/

The official Web site of the Monarchy in Britain provides a fascinating look at royal life throughout history and today, including a section on the Tudor Dynasty:

http://www.royal.gov.uk./index.htm

Many Web sites and search engines provide information and links on broader topics in history. One example is a Web page called History Resources, a guide to a huge variety of history sites:

http://www.liv.ac.uk/~evansjon/humanities/history/history.html

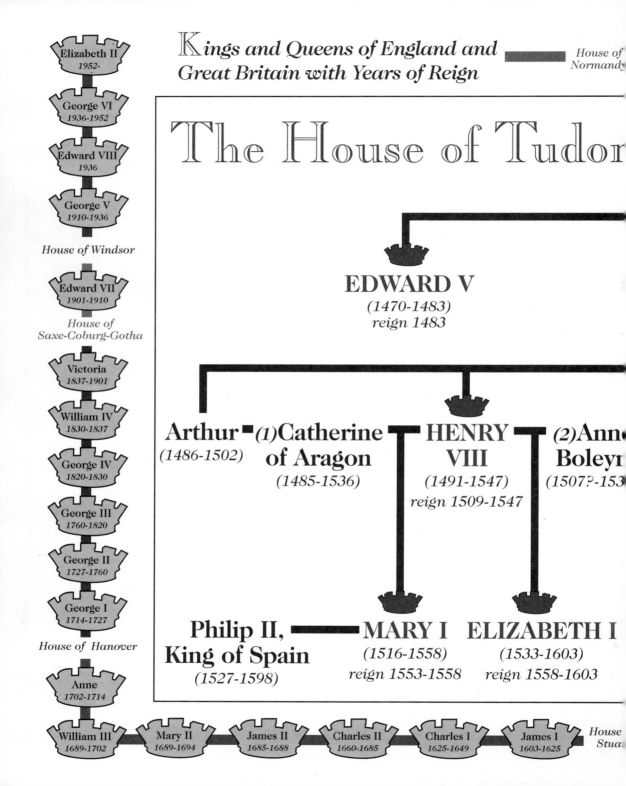

Kings and Queens of England and Great Britain with Years of Reign

House of Normandy

The House of Tudor

House of Windsor
- Elizabeth II 1952-
- George VI 1936-1952
- Edward VIII 1936
- George V 1910-1936

House of Saxe-Coburg-Gotha
- Edward VII 1901-1910

House of Hanover
- Victoria 1837-1901
- William IV 1830-1837
- George IV 1820-1830
- George III 1760-1820
- George II 1727-1760
- George I 1714-1727
- Anne 1702-1714

EDWARD V
(1470-1483)
reign 1483

Arthur (1486-1502) — (1)Catherine of Aragon (1485-1536) — HENRY VIII (1491-1547) reign 1509-1547 — (2)Anne Boleyn (1507?-153[...])

Philip II, King of Spain (1527-1598) — MARY I (1516-1558) reign 1553-1558

ELIZABETH I (1533-1603) reign 1558-1603

House of Stuart
- William III 1689-1702
- Mary II 1689-1694
- James II 1685-1688
- Charles II 1660-1685
- Charles I 1625-1649
- James I 1603-1625

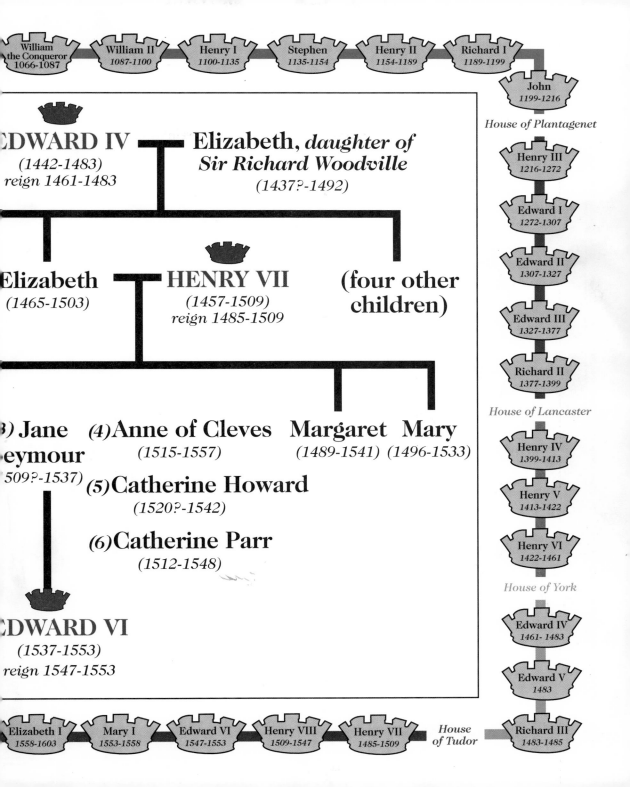

William the Conqueror 1066-1087

William II 1087-1100

Henry I 1100-1135

Stephen 1135-1154

Henry II 1154-1189

Richard I 1189-1199

John 1199-1216

House of Plantagenet

Henry III 1216-1272

Edward I 1272-1307

Edward II 1307-1327

Edward III 1327-1377

Richard II 1377-1399

House of Lancaster

Henry IV 1399-1413

Henry V 1413-1422

Henry VI 1422-1461

House of York

Edward IV 1461-1483

Edward V 1483

Richard III 1483-1485

EDWARD IV *(1442-1483) reign 1461-1483*

Elizabeth, *daughter of Sir Richard Woodville (1437?-1492)*

Elizabeth *(1465-1503)*

HENRY VII *(1457-1509) reign 1485-1509*

(four other children)

3) Jane Seymour *(1509?-1537)*

(4) Anne of Cleves *(1515-1557)*

(5) Catherine Howard *(1520?-1542)*

(6) Catherine Parr *(1512-1548)*

Margaret *(1489-1541)*

Mary *(1496-1533)*

EDWARD VI *(1537-1553) reign 1547-1553*

Elizabeth I 1558-1603

Mary I 1553-1558

Edward VI 1547-1553

Henry VIII 1509-1547

Henry VII 1485-1509

House of Tudor

Index

Page numbers in *italics* refer to illustrations.

About the Author

Robert Green is a freelance writer who lives in New York City. He is the author of *"Vive la France": The French Resistance during World War II* and biographies of important figures of the ancient world: *Alexander the Great, Cleopatra, Hannibal, Herod the Great, Julius Caesar,* and *Tutankhamun,* all for Franklin Watts. He is also the author of biographies of other British monarchs: *Queen Elizabeth I, Queen Elizabeth II, King George III, Queen Victoria,* and *William the Conqueror.*